Blank Sign Book

Anne Lesley Selcer

MEMPHIS
ORDER ONLINE
FedEx

WOLFMAN BOOKS

Wolfman Books
410 13th St.
Oakland, CA 94612
wolfmanhomerepair.com

ISBN: 978-0-9983461-9-9

Blank Sign Book is made possible by Southern Exposure's Art Writing Fellowship. Generous support for Southern Exposure is provided by the David Cunningham Memorial Bequest, the Gelfand Family Foundation, Grants for the Arts/San Francisco Hotel Tax Fund, the National Endowment for the Arts, the Nicholson Family Foundation, the San Francisco Arts Commission Grant Program, the Violet World Foundation, The Andy Warhol Foundation for the Visual Arts, the Zellerbach Family Foundation, and Southern Exposure's members and donors.

SOUTHERN EXPOSURE

Southern Exposure
3030 20th Street
San Francisco, CA 94110
www.soex.org

Distributed by Small Press Distribution spdbooks.org

This project is supported by the Oakland City Council and funded by the City of Oakland's Cultural Funding Program.

BLANK SIGN BOOK

Love is never directed toward this or that property of the loved one (being blond, being small, being tender, being lame), but neither does it neglect the properties in favor of an insipid generality (universal love): The lover wants the loved one *with all of its predicates*, its being such as it is. The lover desires the *as* only insofar as it is *such*—this is the lover's particular fetishism. Thus, whatever singularity (the Lovable) is never the intelligence of some thing, of this or that quality or essence, but only the intelligence of an intelligibility.

–Giorgio Agamben

Time Flows Onto the Highways, Escapes up the Interstate

After police officer Darren Wilson was not indicted for killing teenager Michael Brown in Ferguson, Missouri in 2014, the city burned. All over the country, bridges and highways filled with protest. This photograph of Berkeley's Interstate 80 was taken by a freelance photographer for the Associated Press. As the striking image came up on Facebook, one could nearly hear sharp incredulous intakes of breath. "Beautiful!" unfurled in comment after comment under the image. In the picture, a vertical flow of traffic is held off in both directions. Docile cars point north and south for miles. Inside every car, it is quiet. Outside, on the California highway, the perpetual whir and whoosh of a flow which never ever stops: halted. Inside that silence, inside the cessation of productive time, a different scale of noise, a row of human bodies.

A photograph is always dead silent, but this photograph contains a different silence. This silence is not the vacuum photography creates as touch, sound, smell and taste defer to sight. It is not the world locked into stillness by the camera's eye. Rather, this stillness has been cast over commuting cars by the horizontal noise of a collective refusal. Bodies freeze the mighty California highway. They stop one of the State's most overwhelming, insidious machineries. In this photograph, the scale of the disruption is seen from above in David versus Goliath proportion. For the people in the streets that night, this aesthetic checkerboard of lights depicted just what was happening: *police are ceaselessly taking Black life, and therefore we want to stop time.*

Response to the racially motivated police killing happened in suburban space. All over the country people disrupted highways, commuter trains and suburban landmarks—the QuikTrip, Beauty Town, Auto Center, the Mobil On The Run. Ferguson residents heavily mocked the word "protest" on Twitter. Instead, *banging on the system* described what came to be called the Ferguson Uprising. Shutting down Interstate 80 was not expressing an opinion, taking a stand, nor showing up to be counted. That moment on the highway was the opposite of representation. In dispersed space, nowhere near a center, Black social life became visible in the live streams on the nightly news.

Frank Wilderson explained in a 2015 lecture[1] that *the citizen* recognizes itself by knowing it is not *the slave.* The libidinal economy is central to the Afro-pessimist theory from which he speaks. Black bodies are not merely rejected in this economy of Eros—rather, the entire economy circulates around their exclusion. "The black body in the trees is what constitutes the white family," he quoted David Marriott. It is impossible to talk about Western beauty—the currency of this economy—without this equation.

All images bear lines of relation with beauty, order and meaning. We are never looking at them without establishing proximity to these things. This beautiful picture sublimates political uprising into a legible articulation for those concerned with justice, itself an image, and an image impossible to imagine without a birds-eye view.

The modernist dream—that form expresses content—is really the most recent reference we have for beauty. Beauty seems incidental here, and therefore "real," as if with one illuminating flash, a photographer has captured the historical present, top down. Its silence collects and amplifies the tensed, heroic feeling of direct action. When this photograph got posted, it looked as if things were "exactly as they appear."

In her lecture "Beauty and Social Justice," Elaine Scarry asserts, "fairness requires a symmetry of all of our relations to one another."[2] But in this decentralized, dematerialized space, bodies rendered formless by capitalism show up outside the political logic of appearance. The agora, that Greek space on which democratic representation is premised, is a forever receding horizon for these bodies. The agora has not only been digitized, dissolved into data owned by corporations, or appropriated by gentrification and neoliberal policy, certain bodies were not ever part of it: slaves, women, non-property owners. And if eventually they gained rights officially, social death, mass incarceration and privatization has historically precluded Western representation as such. Equivalency between subjects in the agora is *always* an image. These problems can be considered inextricable from appearance itself, both in its philosophical sense and in its mandate by representative democracy.

Hito Steyerl troubles the foundation of Western picture space, "Linear perspective is based on several decisive negations…this reinvention of the subject, time, and space was an enabling toolkit for Western dominance of its concepts—as well as for redefining standards of representation, time, and space."[3] These suburban uprisings were not exactly protest. They were not the heroic gatherings now sanctioned by history, in the center of the city where the "people" live. This was a disturbance in the logic structure of appearance. The highway blockades interfered with racist capitalism at the logistical level, atop the monstrous viaduct designed without humans to facilitate human flow. This was a total reversal of the logic of the flâneur.

Frank Wilderson asserts that unlike certain historical atrocities, the violence of social death is *atemporal*. It is not available for representation at all on the picture plane, where justice lives. I scrawled in my notebook, "time flows onto the highways." The fantasy is that the result of the highway being stopped is another kind of time being restarted.

Day and Night

"the house protects the dreamer"
—Gaston Bachelard

Coming into culture is also coming into discipline. It begins with trying to get newborn babies to sleep at night, which they would not otherwise. Simple: night from day. The process of subjectification is palpable, you can trace its progression daily via a series of corrections, separations, instructions. We teach them to be children. There is an argument lurking deeply in here somewhere that art is one level on which politics can shift.

What if, after an infancy and subsequent enculturation into sleeping at night, a person gets flipped by work into an opposite schedule? Then we have another culture. We have a culture that no longer forms, and is no longer formed by an individual body growing up through concentric circles of mother's arms, family, home, neighborhood, village or town, one which no longer resonates with, as Henri Lefebvre says, "days, nights, seasons, the waves and tides of the sea, monthly cycles."[1] Then, what if that body also does not have a bed, but rents one by the shift? What if that body without a bed does not have citizenship, but does not have the proper papers to go home again?

The project began when filmmaker Lynne Sachs, curious about the "shift bed," entered the open, bustling sociality of a Chinese cultural center to ask people their stories. In a small apartment which approximates the spaces where many live, she filmed elders cooking together, eating together, passing time, recounting their lives. Everything here is aesthetically interesting: the music, the color, the variation of surface, the mishmash of personal belongings, the pacing, the intimacy between the economically constituted family of the small apartment. Often, she shot in mirrors to increase light and space among the warren of bunk beds. Interspersed with luminescence and music, the narrative builds from a series of tightly framed portraits. The film is a love song to the human face.

Here, we could talk about the social air of a tiny apartment shared by numerous, unrelated adults, or about the novel, generative collaboration between an experimental filmmaker and Chinatown residents, or we could talk about the profoundly vulnerable population of Chinese elders living in the enclaves of protection and shared language that dot the United States. We could talk about the direct threat posed by the expansion of capital into every interstice of city space, as evidenced in San Francisco by an exponential increase in Ellis Act[2] evictions, of the evicted Lee family[3] who lived in their Chinatown apartment for thirty-four years, in Vancouver by the destruction of the Ming Sun Benevolent Society,[4] and portended by the growing number of art studios in New York's Chinatown. We all know about the rhythm that follows artists around cities. What if we name the source of the shift worker's interruption what it essentially is: another body, with more money? Then there is a new rhythm, a rhythm which emanates from the bodies whose needs are so large that the space of one bed for one dreaming body is unviable. We might place the shift bed upon the same spectrum as the imperative to leave one's home country. We might consider that Lefebvre's concentric rhythms of humanism have always been a dream.

This is an argument that the beauty of the film *Your Day is My Night*—a saturated beauty of texture and proximity, stamped in Chinatown reds and blues, awash in ambivalent New York light—is a palliative beauty. It is impossible to experience filmic love here without also understanding the film is about the recession of the human subject. The film's refrain is the failure of home, of family, of country, of protection itself. Silently, at its center, a bed, the site of dreams, synecdoche for the individual interiority turned commodity.

The artist here has shown us the dream, via the beauty of the individual face, to the quiet, sweet melody of the dream's failure. From this contradiction, I surmise a theory of art's political efficacy in the present: the impulsion is to become very, very small and very hard underneath several layers of total availability, adaptability, flexibility, and precarity, to be infinitely adjustable by location, schedule, and interface. Inside is assumed to be a small core of self, fixed, closed, and perpetually vying for its own survival and individual satisfaction. Against this structural adjustment of self into subject, art remains open—and I don't mean the market which surrounds art, I mean the work of the artist themself who, in lieu of being able to resonate openly with Lefebvre's rhythms, generations, and seasons, relegates their open flow into object-based play, and thus each time re-presents the possibility of an open world, to be accessed through the openness of others. That site of encounter with art is the troubled political efficacy of art in this moment. It is troubled because that dear and representative moment of opening is itself commodified, sanctioned, and sectioned off and the habit of having it, like a porn climax, can stand in for an actually open world.

But I fight on the side of the creator who, against the self's structural adjustment, does this thing, be it alone, in order to be multiple again. Perhaps that is where it becomes relevant that the subject/actors in *Your Day is My Night* eventually became a troupe that performed the script live around New York, and to this day, hang out with the director and go to see films.

However, Yi Chun Cao, Yueh Hwa Chan (Linda), Che Chang-Qing, Ellen Ho, Yun Xiu Huang, Sheut Hing Lee, Kam Yin Tsui still have no real permanent, secure base from which to protect their dreams—and that, of course, is the limitation of art. Art is not a corrective song, perhaps it's even a vestige. But the human body—the beginning point or end point of the rhythm of humanist culture, and that which justifies it—is now overtaken by and dissolved into the rhythm itself. No bed, for some, no nation. The film ends with this Federico García Lorca poem:

> Forgetting does not exist, nor dreams
> just raw flesh
> kisses tie our mouths
> in a tangle of new veins.
> Those who hurt will hurt without rest,
> those who fear death will carry it on their shoulders.
> Let there be a panorama of open eyes
> and burning bitter wounds.
> Nobody sleeps in this world.
> No one. No one.
> I said it before.
> Nobody sleeps.

The Plaza

I wasn't at the plaza because my family broke up. I'll put it like that. That weekend, I put on my most beautiful dress and went to a conference about revolution and language. There I saw many writers I met through my husband, who was never actually my husband, but who was supposed to be, the man who I knew two minutes before having a child with, and whom I loved. I loved him, or began to, because he was a socialist from France and socially awkward when the Americans in the living room where we met seemed too sunken into themselves to extend themselves to him. Identity came up at the conference a lot and I suppose this was American identity. So I extended myself to him, and he extended himself to me. I had just arrived home from several years in Canada and was identifying as a socialist then too, and everything and everyone, including the way the Americans talked, felt slow.

I would have been at the plaza with my quick-made husband, but I was in an apartment watching Occupy Oakland on YouTube, having mouthed and written—in a courtroom, a social service cubicle—words spoken to me to describe what had happened in our wooden floored kitchen. The words seemed so stupid and cinematic and to need lots and lots of padding before I spoke them, an explanation that I was "highly educated," that I had not been violence's victim but rather, its refuser. There is a well-shaded part of me which wonders about never having been given the official description of what happened in our kitchen. I would like to be able to write, "words call forms into being" but I cannot, quite.

The not-husband would have been at the plaza with me. He would have been happy, and telling everyone with nationalistic pride—even if his racist French classmates bullied him, and he was the first French-born son to a mother who worked in a factory all week—how they do it at protests in France. I suppose this is identity too. Instead, I was watching flash-bang grenades and teargas clouds on a screen in my kitchen, mostly alone, after days of teaching my child to speak, paint, and ride a trike, having lost my teaching job at the for-profit art college, and going to work selling expensive dresses at a shop down the street which would soon close for lack of business.

I got on the train with my two year old and went on the Port of Oakland shutdown.

I swung the baby carrier around to the back for the five-mile march.

I took the train alone to Poetry for the People, held each Sunday in the plaza at 12, sat alone quietly, then left.

I was treated politely, as I was ever increasingly by the writers I'd met through my not-husband, who were now at the plaza every day, together. I was thinking all the time about what motherhood was keeping me from, but did not have the vocabulary to understand it yet structurally. I felt incredibly buoyed when in at least two pictures of Voina—the bombastic, political art collective from Russia—I spotted a child packed sweetly into her carrier. It wasn't until very recently I realized that the child's mother was likely Nadya from Pussy Riot, famously put in jail in 2012. My new job was our survival, and our survival depended unequivocally on that not happening to me.

The poems I wrote during Occupy were my first poems to contain an "I" in about ten years. The inalienable rights won in preceding revolutions now boiled down to the right to express my feelings. One poem, which I cannot identify as something I would write, has sad feelings. I want to get on the train / to stride down the hill past the strip club lights, deep down into the financial district, then into the shopping district, then into the underground, warm and dirty; / to sit through the noise of the tunnel after the gentrified port, / to sit through the tunnel's decibels pulling towards the clamor of five thousand people, / to pull past the failed development where there are houses but no grocery stores, / into the center of town, the other town, / which is not exactly the other town but not exactly another town, a town adjacent; / I want to think about being adjacent, symbiosis, resource use, resource drain. / I will not get on the train. / I will nurse my child, light a candle, read the news. Wooden floor, high rent, the spirit left clamoring East with all my friends, / I want to get on the train.

I recently searched out a good description of *agora*, the ancient Greek gathering in the city plaza, upon which democracy is premised: *The agora constituted human life as a novel and autonomous form. The concern of the polis was to make the world appear as fully as possible by enabling every free man to take a stance.*[1] To this, I ask how can the female appear at the agora when her whole public history has been one of either overexposure or privatization, either a figure appropriated by the aesthetic, or formless resource reproducing everyday life in a series of non-waged obligations? A child is a private matter in the United States. In San Francisco, daycare costs as much as rent. Without man nor money, I was off the grid, and that showed up as a wrong morality in most of my interactions. The ecstatic feelings of fostering a brand new life, the ambitious plans of a proud parent, the personal graduation into motherhood all got lugged behind me into a social service office. There, under florescent lights, our lives were reduced to an economic problem. Now I realize that aside from my frequent physical absence from gatherings and events, something else also happened. I sank below a line, below a line which communicates. I could talk, I could do my hair, put on makeup, show up. But I was not in full relation. It came up at the conference tentatively: the connection between not having the time to participate in Occupy, and being actually disenfranchised. I thought of the traumatic texture of everyday life for Oakland's constantly policed, structurally antagonized populations, mostly African American, who themselves are forced into the representations of antagonism.

I was going to begin this essay, "I will find a way to appear my invisibility into everything I write." The idea, more visual than anything, was about erasure poetics, the coming forth of articulation which is always also hiding, masked. I saw a woman recite a poem once in which, stuttering, most of the words never fully came out. More than my personal problems, I was thinking about the National Security Agency and the Northern California Regional Intelligence Center and our forced, compulsory appearance in the current, bastardized agora.

When I consider the political will of the disenfranchised, I think about spirit, what is not materially there. I think about how resuscitating its form may begin with finding a new shape with the mouth, through the breath, to inflect "housing is a right." In Canada, I often encountered indignation which referenced a previous reality, real or not, *housing is a right, so why is it not being treated as such?* It is easy to look at the violence with which Occupy Oakland was attacked and see it as directly related to Occupy's disinvestment from normative channels of political speech, speech channeled into clear, representative form, intelligibly advocating for its position on a fair field. It is easy to understand the way Occupy Oakland showed up in the cameras as a function of the cameras themselves, of the intense and all-pervasive separation and mediation upon which American social life is premised. If intellectually I worry over the physicality of Occupy, I mean the dogged physicality of Americans (as if *your* feelings could push politics into happening), I also understand it as the return, the flash which illuminated what has been forced into spirit back into the realm of the sensible. Also, it does not matter how I see it intellectually—those feelings came together in the plaza.

Days alone, lack of city squares, work schedules, the precedent of a privatized life, daily habits of violence, a city built for circulation of goods, laptop cafés, endless technologies of mediation. I was separated by four train stops from the plaza while my child slept and my body flexed, alone in the apartment, toward Oakland. At this point, invisibility is an interest and an aesthetic. It has to do with resisting the spirit of vision altogether, its flattening effect, its ordering effect, its stupid way of knowing things, when each encounter is one of difference, identificatory, seeking to know instead of already knowing...and that was Modernization, but still we search, hit enter, search that out. From poet Sean Bonney:

"The forming of the five senses is a labor of the entire history of the world down to the present." Marx describes the smooth transmutation of human love into stone, metal, money, information and power (the five senses of capital). The possibilities of statement that [Amiri] Baraka would seek to embody in his poem attempt a block on that trajectory, seeking to show that those senses were built from stolen materials, and that they have in any case been violently limited by the forces of capitalist need. In a recent essay Baraka has suggested that the limitation to five senses was produced by capitalist alienation, and that there may be infinite sense, reaching backward and forward into time "in modes, forms and directions that we do not even know exist." It is at this point that Marx and Rimbaud can be read together: the derangement of the senses, the derangement of "all" the senses, is the derangement of the "labour of the entire history of the world down to the present."[2]

<u>In Reversal of Appearing</u>

The plaza is filled with screens, the plaza is filled with pictures. What goes in the absence of a plaza. Sunshine then shadows.

Then ten people, a hundred people, a thousand people, a hundred thousand people fill the plaza. Then ten people, a hundred people, a thousand people, a hundred thousand people hold up a representation. Then ten people, a hundred people, a thousand people, a hundred thousand people stream from the plaza, an agora emptying toward the sun.

In the city in which each communication is already artifact / in the city in which each house is luckier / breathing numbers / in the city in which the city does not exist.

Now the plaza is empty, mute with sun. Then instead of a crowd of 100,000 people, you have 100 crowds of 1,000 people. Then instead of 100 crowds of 1,000 people, you have 10,000 crowds of 10 people.

Here, ten people, a hundred people, a thousand people, a hundred thousand people on screen, become window, renamed for absence. Here, a mother holds up a child turned placard, turned window, turned screen, become sign: a renamed plaza.

At the plaza, a line of men advances. At the plaza, elders sell cooking oil, boxes of cereal. At the plaza, the agora rendered visible in the Northern California Regional Intelligence Center sensors. Sensing reversed, the senses redacted, the redacted rhythm of a plaza.

In which / the plaza was always a representation / turned to look / in the city in which / each house is luckier, breathing numbers / in the city in which / a hundred thousand messages amass and riot / in the city in which / a shadow recomposes identically over every redistribution of forms / in the city in which / the city does not exist / turned to look and my city was gone / at the plaza / the noise of its absence.

"20.—Turn around and the sky opens its mouth. You have disappeared among us. This is a book that does not exist. We've got you surrounded. Sky and death. Sky and blood. Perfection and pain. We are yours when you believe you're devouring us. We are yours with our mouths closed. Instruments of your phonation. We do not differentiate. We jump through the hoop of the sky. We are space and we are surface. The sky has a body that walks. The path has been covered in blood."

We cover our girlish faces. We are the war.

"In the absence of a licit space for the captive female's desire, it, too, becomes engulfed as crime."
—Saidiya V. Hartman

I began to write: Style *by Dolores Dorantes slashes fuchsia through structures of totalitarian authority and gendered domination. A swarm of girls declares, not without Eros, that outermost fastener to sociality first to be disturbed, dismantled, deactivated, deadened or rerouted by overt acts of domination and the prosaic paths of power, "We will blossom without your consent." This blossoming makes war, or is war—"We are the fresh fruits of war." The liveliness of these girls shoots way up beyond any concept of "survival." Their efficacious energy volleys violence back in the language of desire.* My theory there, swimming up through slick black obsidian black light obliterating black ruffled feathers of traumatic experience, is that survivors of social violence get their social radiance disturbed, their social legibility obscured. The very thing which connects, communicates, exchanges, seeks out, and secures inclusion in the networks necessary for survival—self-possession—is challenged. Taking away a person from their body casts that person out from the social world, even if just for a moment. We could conceive of *Style* as a dress cinching the absolute abjection of social vanquishment with the perfect waist-defining sash: a way to clothe bare life.

> "8.—We came to visit your bed. A cluster of girls. Everything was very ambiguous. Everything was bloodless. We came. To approach you. To find your hands ready for torture. To stain you for when you wake. We are a cluster of girls playing at kissing each other. Taking you by the hands. Dazzle. We aren't doing anything bad. We are not pain not exhaustion not death."

This insurgent book can be contextualized within the phenomenon of femicide (or feminicide)[1] in Juárez, Mexico. That is defined as gender-based murder, and cannot be separated from US economic domination of Mexico and control of its border. In Juárez, maquiladoras occupy a legalistic liminal zone near the border, unprotected by labor rights. Dorantes worked as a journalist there; she wrote *Style* just after her subsequent exile. The book rebounds with vitality stolen by transnational domination and the subsequent chaotic drug economy. "We will blossom fruits of blood. Trees of ash."

Saidiya Hartman writes that *seduction* during slavery is exploited as an "alchemy that shrouds direct forms of violence under the 'veil of enchanted relations.'" She goes on, "The intimacy of the master and slave purportedly operated as an internal regulator of power and ameliorated the terror indispensible to unlimited domination."[2] The narrators of *Style* speak back from this imposed predicament using their own needs, desires, and undead or unkillable libidinal energies to plot the ending. In supernatural anti-lyric, they beg and sexually threaten a male authority, intoning enough power to overcome his life. This can be read as a style of survival and a fighting style which leverages domination's force like a boomerang.

> "14.—Give us a bottle and let's be done with your world. Light us up and the fire will spread like a plague. We arrive at your office. At your machine. We arrive at your teacher's chair. At that world that is no longer the world. Where nothing touches and we kiss each other. We join our girlish lips damp with some kind of fuel. Give us a forest. Give us the presidency."

In Juárez, the femicides are ritualistic, horrific, and accompanied by sexual violence. From *Terrorizing Women: Feminicide in the Americas,* "Violence is aggravated under permanent or temporary conditions of social exclusion and situations of dependence or of minimal or nonexistent citizenship for women." Any representation of femicide is potential spectacle. Race intensifies this phenomenon. Rita Laura Segato's work avoids this. As she explains, the narcos (or drug traffickers) challenge the Mexican government for sovereign power over the territory and population of Juárez, "The victim's control of her body space is expropriated. For this reason, it can be said that rape is the act par excellence of Carl Schmitt's definition of sovereignty: unrestricted control; arbitrary and discretionary sovereign willpower...In the language of feminicide, the female body also signifies territory...the woman's body is annexed as part of the nation that is conquered."[3]

Style's taunting, sexual, and threatening lyric of white-hot energetic overcoming conjures new lexicons for surviving. There is that word—survival—here meaning literal survival, but always also pointing to the murderous potential of any interpersonal or sexual violence. Poet and artist Cassandra Troyan writes, "Post-sovereignty is then an image of the subject who has already been killed—brutalized through illness, poverty, sexual violence, white supremacy, colonialism, genocide, misogyny and suicide—but refuses to die...a body of resistance, bodies of refusal, bodies which say—*you have killed me but I am still not dead.*"[4]

Dorantes draws upon the awful cultural storehouse of images of the (beautiful, female) victim. But her scapegoat does not ask for a Levinasian look which depends on another to say, *yes, you are human, I grant you recognition with my gaze*. In this performative revenge lyric, the lyrical 'I' is a feminine swarm, a dissimulating mass, and the 'you' is a male authority. The book seethes with exhilarated, otherworldly, post-human resentment which draws energy from social forms—beauty, fetishized femininity, formalized sexual play—to enact a spell for the once-killed to regain liveliness. Force is a foundational structure of the West's self-reproduction and thus archived in the Western imaginary. Playing with its lexicon can enable one to cope with power, to be, as Lauren Berlant says, "a mass of incoherent things and not be defeated by that." She asserts, "Training in one's own incoherence, training in the ways in which one's complexity and contradiction can never be resolved by the political, is a really important part of a political theory of non-sovereignty." In this thinking, art is delinked from worldmaking, yet grounded in the political.

Trauma is a Memory Palace with the Roof Blown Off

I arrive in the heat of the Mediterranean summer in Venice at the Canadian Pavilion and find a saturated stage set, a memory theater. I feel I have been here before, except in a part of San Francisco which replicates a Mediterranean town—the Italian quarter, North Beach, where the San Francisco Art Institute nestles upon a steep hill. Canadian artist Geoffrey Farmer was an exchange student there in the 1990s and thirty years later rebuilt the school's fountain here in Italy, a ridiculous ejaculate of water tossing high into the trees of the Venice Biennale. I watch children and tourists—who moments ago were fashionable, travel-resourced art lovers and professionals—laughing and cooling off. Water is everywhere! At odd intervals, the exuberant white jet flies willy-nilly through the hole in the roof of the pavilion. Its jouissance defiles and defies decorum. Water shoots in thin spurts from the ground, from a rigged plant, from the trunk of the single tree (somehow), and from a mad cuckoo clock which echoes

Vancouver's history-fetish Steam Clock in the artist's hometown. Water razzes people, touches them, plays with them and cools them off. This is tactile, comedic aesthesis. I venture outside to gather myself in front of the artist's statement; as I read, I am tickled or kissed by a tiny rogue spurt of water.

In approximately thirty days, I will be back in the Bay Area reading Chris Kraus's brand new autobiography of writer Kathy Acker, "So there were two I's in the book, the I without the parentheses and the I within the parentheses." At a party in Vancouver approximately ten years prior, Geoffrey Farmer told me how, twenty years prior, he sat in Acker's San Francisco Art Institute classroom as she *strode into the classroom and put her boots up on the table*. I have imagined that precise moment many times since with jealousy and lust, too young to have been one of the tattooed "wild girls" Kathy admired who arrived to class on motorcycles.

Two days after walking through the Canadian Pavilion, I will meet cousin Miriam for lunch in Berlin. Miriam's grandfather perished, she explains over Niçoise salads, in a camp in Siberia where he was deported after the family's protective Swiss passports were nullified under Hitler's regime. He died before Miriam's birth. Her own father—who as a child, depending on who you ask, stayed on a farm on the outskirts of Berlin or hid in a forest for the balance of the war, and whom my own grandmother unsuccessfully tried to bring overseas to safety—felt perpetual trauma over the absence of any site at which to mourn. Forty years prior to the lunch, a child Miriam solved this dilemma in a dream by finding her grandfather's body. In the days following the lunch, I will consider getting the grandfather's name tattooed on my arm where the internment camp numbers went. A monument, a marker, a plaza, a pavilion. Memory is vernacular, and it follows that history is the memory of the State. Outside the Canadian Pavilion, whilst kissed by a funny little spurt of water, I read, "the struggle for the removal of the Canada sign; if it is still on the front of the pavilion, I lost." Thirty days after the lunch, I will pore over the family tree to discover that in order to get the tattoo, I will have to choose between four disparate spellings of the family name.

Twenty years prior, upon reading Beckett for the first time, I dreamed about death. In this dream, death is a grandfather blown to pieces at the side of a road, a body become matter. Inside the perfect replica of the San Francisco Art Institute fountain, there are seventy-one replicas of the seventy-one planks of wood which flew off the artist's grandfather's lumber truck at the time of his deadly 1955 collision with a train. The artwork is called *A way out of the mirror*. It is a line from Allen Ginsberg's poem "Laughing Gas" from *Kaddish and Other Poems*, 1961. In austere raised bronze, an excerpt by this anti-monumental poet appears at the entrance to the installation. Nearly the whole top of the Canadian Pavilion has been removed in the making of the piece, and upon feeling my own inherited trauma to be finally fastened to a place, a name, I scribble in a notebook, "trauma is a memory palace with the roof blown off."

Reading

Her murmuring, her mumbling, accented. Her skin, her freckles, her glasses, crisp paper. The *her* of writing, whomever. The written word is like currency in that, like money's correspondence to value, there remains no attachment between the hand of the writer and the words written, and certainly not the mouth. Writing is an act of mark making.

The Otolith Group recorded poet and painter Etel Adnan reading from *Sea and Fog*, her book of lyrical sentences built into short, vivid blocks. The video is part of the collective's trilogy on the politics of water. Etel's physical presence is tightly framed by the camera and shot in close detail, never straight on. She sits at a wooden table and reads out loud. Her boy's haircut, her thick round glasses, her aged skin texture the film. In one sequence the camera waits quietly as her thumb pauses in the book. Light from a window brightens. The page hovers mid-air with indecision. This is thinking, filmed. Time feels antique, material as paper.

I See Infinite Distance Between Any Point and Another[1] was shot in her Paris apartment among old rugs, wooden chairs, canvases leaning against a hallway wall, paints. These surfaces have a resonance thick as Adnan's French-English, which occasionally renders what she is reading just beyond intelligibility. A copy of Hölderlin, a quill pen, a green patch of paint with a crack, presumably a detail of one of her paintings. In *The Acoustic Mirror*, Kaja Silverman says, "The notion that cinema is able to deliver 'real' sounds is an extension of that powerful Western episteme...which identifies the voice with proximity and with the here and now—of a metaphysical tradition which defines speech as the very essence of presence." If writing is always an absence, a convexity, pointing elsewhere, Adnan's body becomes a stand-in for that which her writing transmits. The recorded sound of her voice makes her presence palpable. Meaning reverberates around the text like sound reverberates around the body. The sip of water is recorded on the same aural plane as the voice. The act of filming is tangible; we feel the quotidian details of mediation. If writing bypasses orality, reading aloud resurrects something that exceeds the voice. The rhythm of reading aloud, distinct from the rhythm of speaking, contains a has-been, a telling, reaching into permanence, then reenacting it. "When the voice is identified in this way with presence, it is given the imaginary power to place not only sounds but meaning in the here and now. In other words, it is understood as closing the gap between signifier and signified," says Silverman. Writing always mimes truth telling; the voice confirms its veracity.

At the poetry reading, we are not witnessing authority as it is handed down via the mouth of *he who speaks*, we are being moved in the sequencing rhythm of another law. At a reading, we see a writer remaking an act that arose by the multidimensional complexities of thinking, impulse, mimicry, emotion, and transfer to written mark. We see this complexity coming back through the body. If, as Barthes says, the text is remade through silent reading, the "other law" of writing is rebirthed at the poetry reading. We hear writing's phantasmagorical texture as a live, thinking art set loose from the linear dictates of the page. The voice's multitude of frequencies—transmitted silently to paper during writing, echoing while the reader is in the book—get resurrected. The body of the writer becomes significant in the moment when it comes into the collective body. Here, subjectivity is merely a beginning place from which to enter into communication, "The voice is the site of perhaps the most radical of all subjective divisions—the division between meaning and materiality...it is situated 'in the partition between the biological body and the body of language, or, if one prefers, the social body.'"

This camera records this body with so little distance—the wrinkle of the neck, hair wisp, a confluence of freckles—that it becomes *whatever singularity.*[3] This body does not stand in for the desire of the viewer. It is not on display, it is one texture among the others—the texture of her paintings, her rugs. "The sonorous envelope of the mother's voice is a fantasy of origins..." writes Silverman, yet here a woman's voice speaks for itself, reads its own text, originates art. Now we know her voice and body—as we know, for instance Hemingway's mass—and in the way that we know very few bodies of female artists. Filled with itself, presencing.

I See Infinite Distance fills absence with resonance. It is a love letter to mediation, a détournement of the record. There is a doubled, archival care: Etel holding her words about the sea, the camera holding her presence as she holds them. Our eyes hold all of it. Here, the image creates a full circuit between the absent writer and the reader, inside of which the text is alive. At the end a frozen sea cracks, painfully, slowly. It is not a metaphor. This is film's ability to place the real and the remediated on the same plane. It is not an aesthetic image, it redirects Adnan's reading back into the world.

VOLUME ONE
1931-1934

Edited and with an
Gunther St

$3.25 A HARVEST/HBJ BOOK

Love

I grew up on Anaïs Nin. For all that one can say about this highly narcissistic French woman of Spanish origin who wrote mediocre surrealist texts for which she is less known, and decent, straight-forward "erotica" for a dollar a page, for which she is more known, Nin was a woman whose life was guided by Eros. At age 15, in the backseat of a local boy's car, I admired the cover design of *Ladders to Fire* which was small press Modernist redux circa late-1950s. I borrowed the book and proceeded to fall heavily under its influence. It was the first experimental novel in her *Cities of the Interior* series, books which became for me objects of heretofore unknown beauty. I read them as artifacts—of Paris in the '20s, of some prototypical bohemia. They were the origin of the long, undulating sentence (I'd had yet to find Woolf) taken back up in the work of Cixous and Irigaray (and early Lisa Robertson), of the mixed media book, of the long poem, and of the singular charm of small press cover design. They marked a personal inculcation into love, sex, and the subject versus object conundrum, all beginning appropriately in the backseat of a teenage boy's car.

Nin, aside from being obsessed with her own image, was obsessed (a word used twice here in homage to her cadence which ever bore the mark of her muse) with Freud. The main problem of her life and literature was the reinstatement, as she would characterize it, of the unconscious—all that was fluid, feeling, "feminine," underground—into, well, everything. Her life was project and product of her work (funded by her banker husband) and this work manifested in the championing, childing, feeding, housing and loving of several artists. Nin's conception of love was as a counter current to the conditions produced by the specialization and industrialization of Modern Paris. She repeated the Romantic gestures of noblesse to distinguish herself, just in the black tights and dark lipstick of Modernist bohemia.

Nin might have defined love as the softening of what is hard and the connecting of what is disconnected. This definition reiterated Romanticism's longing for reconnection with the ether: the lost maternal voice which, cloudlike and soft, surrounded the baseness of the imminent world. Freud was her way back, specifically her misreading of the unconscious as benevolent. Of course, the world of fluid interiority enacted in Nin's prose manifested the desire for ultimate connection, oceanic connection, final connection, a desire which scantly deviated from the Romantics' model of transcendence. Where the ontology of one produced writing that constantly sought the ethereal in the material, wistfully evidencing the "fall" from Spirit in bits of earthly beauty, Nin's (in Freudian terms) was a dream of embryonic reconnection—the pain and triteness of individuation alleviated by slips into the surreal (Susan Sontag explicates the impulse elegantly in "Melancholy Objects"). But the concept of the unconscious was so relieving, it seems, that she bathed in its curative powers a little too long, eventually fucking her therapist.

In another era, one might have called Nin an acolyte, but given her proximity to the Modern let's use "narcissist." Of course, her narcissism was of a particular kind—not the outwardly turned, cannibalizing projection of self, capital S, onto a world barely indistinguishable from itself—but a version wherein the self is exceedingly small or hardly there at all. In this scenario, the world, with all its objects and others, are a kind of poetry written semi-consciously by the self. It was a feminine narcissism, the narcissism of the object, one who sees reflection nowhere, but projection (idealized and desired, hardened into thingness) everywhere. It makes sense then Nin should choose for her love object one who gave the impression of being in constant motion—a man capable of moving out of himself into the world, or in this case, constantly, penetratively, into the other—Henry Miller.

Theirs was an odd and perfect pairing. Miller had to know, Nin had to be known. Doubtless, it felt transgressive for each, Miller plunging into the erudite and mannered French haute bourgeoisie, Nin being taken by the dirty American colloquial. The interesting part was the confusion of identity. Henry became a passageway into a world that, by nature of her gender and class, Nin would not have had entry otherwise. There, in the seedy bars and whorehouses of Paris, her visibility as a feminine sign served as a decoy of sorts. Behind it, she conducted research. *Little Birds* and *Delta of Venus* are the result, books of erotica written for the same patron who commissioned Miller for dollar-a-page pornography. Realistically, this corpus surpasses Nin's surrealist novels as her legacy— which essentially is a legacy of female disidentification from sacred sexuality.

Nin had another inadvertent legacy: she built community. Lawrence Durrell, Antonin Artaud, Maya Deren, Edmund Wilson, Djuna Barnes, and many others, connected around her socially and get reconnected through the reportage and gossip of her meandering multi-volume diaries. It was Nin's basic erotic tendency which propelled this connectivity—this desire to move towards, into, with, with love. Of course, decades later, the same impulse was formed by Irigaray and Cixous, Kristeva and others into French feminist poetics.

Emmanuel Levinas distinguishes need from desire as such: needs can be fulfilled, they concern a reproduction of the self. Desire, however moves outward, beyond the self. The first is an animal, fully terrestrial proposition—eating together, sleeping together. Desire transcends this ego-based economy, unfolding the self via the other, after which the world can never be the same. If Nin's love affairs and the majority of her writing sought vigorously to transcend, yet never seem to get beyond her own ego, this general impulse to move outside of the self got carried out in full vitality in her network building. This is all to say: perhaps Nin's broader erotic impulse, the one which created a social world, was the true, productive unfolding. Levinas uses the image of "the face" to describe this phenomenon, and here we have Nin's face on the cover of all the diaries, heavily eyelinered, European, markedly contained. Yet the books are not contained. The characters spill out of the diaries, into her fiction and out into the living world; they are scattered all through literary and art history, and get permanently linked by her cultural map, one which would be eventually retraced in the bedroom of a late 20th century teenager. This is Nin's persistent desire, unfolding.

SHOUT OUT TO MY URBAN
ANGELS SEARCHING FOR POST OR
PRE-GENITAL DESIRE VIA GPS

LIKE SNOT. MUCUS, CUM, SHIT,
SWEAT-THE UNITING
ELEMENTS THAT FORM
THE BASIS OF REALITY

CLOTHING AS AN EXTENSION
OF FLESH

Being Desire

Juliana Huxtable's book *Mucus In My Pineal Gland* kneels to the internet's largesse, struggles with it like a mother. Inside this struggle: the birth of her sexuality and the body horror of femininity with its projection planes and infinite play—also, dysphoria, blackness, fetish, queer sex. The book memorializes the internet—that two-way gazing machine, that ultimate screen, constituting and constitutive of self, Self, Selfie—in loud clanking blue letters. Huxtable's *Mucus In My Pineal Gland* soothes and beautifies the eyes. It has canary yellow endpapers and section dividers of full-sail blue. In blue ink and all caps, the book thins the tiltingly thinning line between "send" and "publish." Framed (or set upon a plinth) like this, Huxtable narrativizes and analyzes an entrée into the new digital sociality layered in reappropriated codes and reused vernaculars, so much representation and infinite language. She permanently time stamps the ephemerality of screen text. She does not line this labyrinth with golden thread, yet never lets go of a productive cynicism—critical of tech corporations and lit sharply with the traumas of race, transmisogyny, and gender normativity.

Let's try this: The self is outside now, held in one hundred or one thousand communication receptors—a face, a pout of lips, light on legs and pointed toes, sent / received. The self is social as ever in its isolation to work, screen, its own personal domestic economy; the domestic realm is punctured by images galore, superabundant info, and sooo much language. As much as the internet is the agora, the polis, the marketplace, the café, the club, the gallery and the library—now all accessible from within the bedroom—it is an apparatus for producing the self. We can no longer talk about the self, we need to talk about the selfie. Because the self has been ensorcelled by the screen. Because social life is in the midst of a dramatic reorganization both materially and conceptually, and the main medium of this reorganization is a gigantic representation machine which is also a gargantuan gazing machine. Because we carry subjectivity in our pockets, office equipment on our backs. I want to call it the internet, but it is more like what the internet makes possible: a complex matrix of the tech industry, the stock market, credit scoring, YouTube likes, twitter bots and of course, social media. "If the primary tool of biopolitics was the census, perhaps we can consider the paradigmatic tool of necropolitics to be the algorithm," says Micha

Cárdenas.[1] It's not new. It is the acuminated tip of modernism tagging or labeling an already-sorted world. On a different artist, I wrote, "To imagine the self in a box, as an icon, setting preferences, adding friends, sharing links, being redirected, seeking out jobs and friends and lovers and apartments…is to continually frame and reframe binaries of ugliness and beauty, blackness and whiteness, the abject and the body, the human and the less-than-human."[2]

Mucus In My Pineal Gland takes on media's power to constitute our desires and ways of seeing and being. From inside a digital glow born of office equipment and total access, it traces an account of survival, clarity, and jouissance. Huxtable expounds upon her pleasure, writes "from the body." This écriture transféminine writes a body in transition, one surviving white supremacy complexly, a body inextricable from layers of power and aesthetic signs. Race, class, and cis privilege do not emanate from selfie art, they are inherent to the medium of looking, to Western aesthetics. Here they are backlit and thrown into stark relief courtesy of Apple. Inside the screen, in the bedroom, dancing with oneself, desire cut free from the (male) Artist's hand, and also dependent on the *sensus communis* of (white) male desire.

▪ ▪ ▪

BREAST BUTTER SOFT,
GLOSSY GLASSY

BUT I SPEAK WELL,
THEY CALL ME ASHLEY

THEN I CALLED ON GOD,
HE CALLED ME ASHY

Selfie art practices reverse Kant's abnegated lust, his concept of "disinterested beauty." They are desire, being desire. Structurally similar to feminist performance practices of the '70s and '80s, selfie poetics master the computer screen grammar of desire, but with a publishing/posting rate one hundred times faster. They radiate digital glamour. Hito Steyerl speaks back to Kant,

> The observer has lost his stable position. There are no parallels that could converge at a single vanishing point. The sun, which is at the center of the composition, is multiplied in reflections...At the sight of the effects of colonialism and slavery, linear perspective—the central viewpoint, the position of mastery, control, and subjecthood—is abandoned and starts tumbling and tilting, taking with it the idea of space and time as systematic constructions.[3]

More than inverting the politics of the white man's

pleasure, that which every artist who is not a white man has to deal with, Huxtable's writing enacts desire cut loose—a force, an intensity, that power inextricable from power,[4] inextricable from resource, race, and gender dynamics, and from the internet. *Feminine* is "one name for what we cannot grasp in established systems of ideas or articulate within the current framework in which the term 'woman' has meaning."[5] Huxtable's work unfolds within this field of possibility. Says Hélène Cixous, "If there is a 'propriety of woman,' it is paradoxically her capacity to depropriate unselfishly…a moving, limitlessly changing ensemble, a cosmos tirelessly traversed by Eros, an immense astral space not organized around any one sun that's any more of a star than the others."[6]

I grappled with whether I could use écriture féminine without a survey of the way it falls short for trans women—with its metaphors of the phallus, of the umbilical cord and intrauterine space—despite its flexibility and claims of anti-essentialism. Ultimately, more than that critique, I felt interested in the fecundity of Huxtable's book. In the way that the aesthetic is always giving birth, one hundred thousand illegitimate and unholy propositions, Huxtable's text and sex—mothered by the internet—soothes and mollifies all of us. Art, the internet, queerness, the feminine monster, "NATAL OVER&&OVERAGAIN."

As a generator of temporality, the vernacular overdetermines any bounded circulation concept or singularity of origin—it moves every-which-way continuously, so an excess or an innovation may erupt at any point, initiating various kinds and intensities and political consequences that can never be predetermined.

Lisa Robertson, *Nilling*

The Communicative Community

...in the spectacle our own linguistic nature comes back to us inverted.
—Giorgio Agamben

What we attempted was an impossible task and it disassembled our community. It pointed us back to the arbitrary category "women," to the limit of our relationships under present political structures, and finally, to the misidentification of what we poets do here in the Bay Area together, pretty much weekly, in private living rooms and nonprofit spaces, at summits and on softball fields, and in tiny afterparties, at formal lectures, at self-organized conferences or university ones, to what happens at our private desks, or propped up in bed or during stolen time at work, on transit, or whilst ignoring the kid, to what happens at the café as every American subject with a laptop also ignores the humans around them, to what gets transmitted or performed or whispered or sung or given as a gift to the rest of us—it pointed us toward our misidentification of that as "community." This is deeply emotional. Insofar as the history of poetry suggests interiority, each week we visited each other's phantasmagorical living rooms—where, with Bay Area real estate, most living rooms double as bedrooms. But our over-intimacy was also doing capitalism's dirty work, caring for each other in a verbal way which did not actually approach lived enmeshment and ultimately was more like an administrative check-in in an exceedingly couch and pillow-lined social space. And not just us. New Yorkers do it, too. Probably others all over the United States. This is what social life looks like between a collection of subjects.

M.M. Bakhtin writes about the carnival as the festival in which the people turn power on its head one day each year, when they burn an effigy of the king. If some of us imagined this is what poetry's reordering of language was doing already, the East Bay Poetry Summit would ramp up this possibility and invite guests. So the summit is when the details of a series of recent assaults came out: a handful of rapes, a push, a hairpull, some domestic violence, a slap. Some of the perpetrators were lesser known to some of us, but some were good friends. Some were letches who we'd been getting consistent misogynist vibes from, but some organized in the center of our community.

Our address to each other took place on a register so direct and activated I am not sure it can be called "conversation." It was infused with disturbing amounts of sunlight, wavering thickly in a bright funnel cloud of fury, lament, debate and militant political desire. More kept coming and more. It spilled over to nonstop email and texts, and so overtook the lives of several Bay Area poets in the summer of 2014. Many of us spent the summer physiologically transformed. The season before, Dia exhibited a Carl Andre retrospective without mentioning Ana Mendieta's death, and Elliot Rodger massacred several UC Santa Barbara students, then left behind a misogynist and racist manifesto. It certainly could not have been a "bad summer" as many began to call it, like the prostitute's euphemism "bad date." It was the summer an active, political, emotional, experimental, critical collection of writers who share anti-capitalist, anti-racist, feminist commitments looked directly into the glare of untouched, entrenched patriarchy.

I have been reading all day about communication, reading around it for months actually, in order to make a case for politics which exceed the horizon of a social justice under current contexts of power: politics beyond representation. When we posted our statement to a website called Pastebin then disseminated it by Facebook, I might have quoted Alphonso Lingis when he states, *the technology that eliminates the noise also eliminates the communication.* I might have uttered, *To designate it, thus, as noise is to conceive it from the point of view of the individual teleologically destined to citizenship in an ideal republic maximally purged of the noise of life and of the empirical domain.* I might have repeated Jodi Dean, *What hinders communication, therefore, is communicability itself: human beings are being separated by what unites them.*

Then, I might have cocked my head to one side, taken the hand of another poet, let her watch my tears well, and murmured Lisa Robertson's words, *The vernacular is movement for which language is not the state, but the condition of emergence of the subject to and for others.* I might have gone back into the streets, returned to the reading, then after chatted excitedly about everything and nothing, and gone on, *It is grammarless rhythm, a mobile, patterned regime of compromise: Something infinitely vulnerable.*

The summer changed our rhythm inexorably and we cannot be the same community. That there was a rhythm to have been changed. That there could be a rhythm between us. That there could be a vernacular life to our open, language-based community, even when the universality of language is what keeps it open, and to persist, its life must precede language or form a language which is specific. That, despite our names, and also necessarily through them, there could be an *us.*

Round

The first time I saw Chris Duncan's sound piece *12 Symbols*, I sat—as audience members were invited to—inside a spacious circle formed by twelve percussionists playing twelve single waist-high cymbals. This iteration of the performance took place in a disused warehouse space on Mare Island, an overgrown outlands where head-high fennel plants throw licorice to the wind. *12 Symbols* whined alive quietly. Twelve bows dragged slowly at the edge of each cymbal to create a low, copper cacophony. Extremely tired, I drifted off for minutes, and awakened faced by an enormous, dark block of sound. One by one, each percussionist had taken up two mallets to strike their cymbal forcefully. Walking in continual rotation, they struck continuously, right then left. Each collision left a long, deep resonance hanging. They played fast. Shimmering layers of sound rose around the circle. Resonance relentlessly piled atop resonance. Soon, the heavy thickness built into an unimaginable, urgent body of noise. The piece lasted around thirty minutes. The simple score created art that grew huge, feral.

Once, I was in the countryside walking through a field of grass, through the normal sounds of insects, wind, sun, green. All at once, I heard a sharp drone, a concert of buzzing. I looked down and small bees were swarming near my feet. The sound surrounded me; its loudness amazed me. A multitude of low tones piled up formidably clipping an enormous racket into the air. The gestures in *12 Symbols* are simple and repetitive. Its power is inherently social. Its maximalism is driven by time; time multiplies the memory of sound, wavering and brassy.

A sonic assertion this large requires a degree of submission or sublimation. It reframes dissonance—which always feels like a kind of threat—as sublime. So I felt my contours, the cold seal my hand formed with the raw floor. *12 Symbols* does not ask for connections, interjections or projections from its listener; everything is offered, all of the energy of this art. The sonic power of *12 Symbols* borrows the resonance of transformation itself, the energy that appears to make time move. The artist cites solar and lunar cycles as influences. Before the piece gradually flamed out, each percussionist increased the speed of drumming considerably, then each laid down their mallets. There was beauty, relief, and the profundity of the transition back into silence, away from this celestial scale of the sound, and back into human space.

A circular composition comprises Janet Cardiff's sound installation *The Forty Part Motet.* Here, human space acuminates into an uncanny assertion of spiritual high beauty. Inside an expansive and cavernous gallery space with polished concrete floors and warehouse windows (sailboats knocking together beyond them), the complex sixteenth-century choral composition *Spem in Alium* emanated from forty small, rectangular, ear-high speakers. Thought to be the pinnacle of early English music, this song braids the voices of eight five-member choirs. In a complex round, they toss Latin phrasings back and forth. Art made by this many voices is a high feat of humanism, and is easily understood as having aesthetic (if historical) value. In the early twenty-first century, this felt like a vestigial kind of pleasure to be taking in an art space.

Cardiff's *The Forty Part Motet* was spectacularly sculptural when heard from the middle of the room. I walked along the edge of the circle of speakers and pressed an ear to each. Each of *the forty* speakers created an intimate aural frame around a singer's singular voice. I had rare, precious access to the inimitable breath, skill, tenor, timbre, tone, and texture, and all the unnamable qualities one hears in a human voice. The experience was technically stunning, but also profoundly intimate, as if each voice in isolation was singing to me. In *The Coming Community*, Giorgio Agamben describes "singularity":

> Love is never directed toward this or that property of the loved one (being blond, being small, being

> tender, being lame), but neither does it neglect the properties in favor of an insipid generality (universal love): The lover wants the loved one *with all of its predicates*, its being such as it is. The lover desires the *as* only insofar as it is *such*—this is the lover's particular fetishism. Thus, whatever singularity (the Lovable) is never the intelligence of some thing, of this or that quality or essence, but only the intelligence of an intelligibility.[1]

In Western culture, "voice" is a metaphor to describe "presence" in a political sense; it has a connotation which is analogous to "will." In a recent lecture, philosopher Jacques Rancière contrasted language with the "cry of animals," which can only express pleasure or pain.[2] According to Rancière, "politics" happens when the impossible becomes possible—that is, when "noisy animals" are perceived to have a position. In contrast, singularity—less a representation of the self, more like an irreducible distillation—suggests a different possibility. Again, art historian and theorist Kaja Silverman, "The voice is the site of perhaps the most radical of all subjective divisions—the division between meaning and materiality…situated 'in the partition between the biological body and the body of language, or, if one prefers, the social body.'"[3] When each singular voice sang from its given speaker, it felt like contact, connection. Just as a photograph of a human face evokes desire, fascination, protection, affection, listening closely to a human voice—especially one at the height of its skill and reaching toward the sublime—feels like a particularly human gift, if not the human gift. Along with the various other listeners, I moved around the circle, eavesdropping on something indefinable and radically irreducible.

The video installation *The Visitors* by Ragnar Kjartansson plays with singular and collective voices. The piece was shown in a darkened room lined by several screens. Vivid on each, a different room of a house, and a single musician playing there: a cellist, a guitarist, a pianist, a banjo player. They are plugged into mics and recording equipment. Each musician hears the others through earphones. They collectively sing a repetitive folk song adapted from a poem written by Ásdís Sif Gunnarsdóttir. The poem-song is plodding, slow, and emotive. "Once again…I fall into…my feminine ways" repeats, then repeats, and repeats. The work is durational, and as the light begins to die around the musicians, crickets start to sing.

Pleasure is dominant in the environment, which is a borrowed mansion. Each room/screen is set up like a Dutch still life, replete with antiques, rich textures, and gorgeously patterned upholsteries framing each musician. It was wonderful to observe the musicians steeped in skill, responding to others out of frame. They are sometimes clad in lingerie, sometimes in a bubble bath, sometimes smoking while pounding a piano, sometimes strumming a guitar on the edge of a bed in which a naked woman is contoured sleepily under a thin sheet. This is all a delicious reference to a 1960s fantasy of freedom and bohemia. The song builds for a full sixty-four minutes. Its old-timey ramble underlines the languid aesthetic. The earnestness of each of the musicians becomes truly beautiful when they sing together separately, and then eventually get up from their individual rooms and tumble, stumble, pop a bottle of champagne, and find each other in the drawing room, or out on the porch, where a sloped, curved friendship alights upon all their shoulders and upon all of us.

Inside the enclosed installation space, we were invited to feel the *being-together* depicted on screen. The piece is deeply nostalgic. What is evoked is like a gorgeous commodity: communalism, singing collectively, the inherent value of one's unique voice. The *personhood* of the voice is revered. The work seethes with individualism but contains the spirit of camaraderie—a coming together as a band of musicians, outliers, and artists. Folk is brought into the gallery space; everything is fluid, spontaneous, celebratory. In contrast to *The Forty Part Motet*, *The Visitors* frames informality. In this dear and enviable temporary utopia, each subject brings their own voice, masters their own instrument, is accepted in their quirks and clothing choices. The multi-gendered crew is free to sing about their "feminine ways." If *The Visitors* enacts a bohemian exceptionalism made possible by a certain set of twentieth-century, first-world conditions, one that is often naturalized as an ideal in the San Francisco Bay Area, it might be worth noting this artist is Icelandic. What we relish about this piece—its apparent spontaneity and earnestness—is its design to evoke a specifically epochal love and longing specific to an era.

Each of these sound-based artworks constitutes subjectivity differently. *12 Symbols* subjects listeners to the mightiness raised by the simultaneous percussive use of repetition, sound waves, and time. *The Forty Part Motet* starts with collective perfection but zooms out to frame the subjective singularity of the voice. *The Visitors* reveres the voice, relieves it from its loneness but not its uniqueness. The collectivity Kjartansson creates restates and reinstates the sanctity of the individual voice against the modern horrors brought by the radical shift to the factory. It posits the aesthetic itself against the dehumanizing automation of life. As emotionally powerful as this move feels, especially raised in languorous song, the more pressing tension today is the algorithm: those sets of data that base their very power on harnessing that which is *most* individual about our individuality—the measurements of our facial features in relation to one another, biometric iris recognition, and especially the voice.[3]

During the Occupy protests of 2011, *resonance*, *sound*, and *musicality* were often words used to describe the spread of revolutionary information between disparate masses. This language reflected a magical begetting, as if something could be made from nothing. As power increasingly asserts itself through biopolitical means, adding layers of risk and precarity to the most basic human contingencies—water, air, shelter, food—unlimiting the possibilities of the senses is one way self, subject, and collectivity can continue to be reworked. When I began to write, I unwittingly began in manifesto mode. I scrawled, "The useless apocalypse of *12 Symbols* is a rehearsal for art which is non-productive but transformative"; I wanted art with that much largess. I attended another performance of the piece. Not from emotion nor content, my eyes began to produce a significant amount of tears. I have no sonic science for this. This is not social change, but it is impossible to deny it is change.

What Imaginary Thing is a Museum?

"But to take our sadness, our fragile courage and our anxiety to the museum every day..."[1]

Two distinct rooms in two different Bay Area museums in 2017 displayed the work of two major artists, one of whom killed the other. One was male and one was female, one was born in Havana in 1948 and one was born in Quincy, Massachusetts in 1935. One exhibited work at the Guggenheim, one won the Rome prize. One, Carl Andre, was famously acquitted for the murder of the other, Ana Mendieta, to whom he was married, and with whom he fought loudly in 1985 just before she fell 34 stories to her death. The ruling was based on insufficient evidence and countered by many facts. The acquittal is not accepted by Mendieta's family and friends, nor by many curators, art lovers and artists. This tragedy continues to hold resonance for many people, but museums and galleries still support Andre's work.

Nothing we can say, think, or write about Mendieta's work now can be fully apart from the facts of her death. Her work has been described as having a "traumatic mood."[2] And yet, Mendieta's art was playful, queer, grotesque, campy, challenging, and not easily readable. She was an artist who played constantly with what her face and body signified, as well as with the body's elemental, non-signifying presence. Her films in the retrospective *Covered in Time and History* radiate the core vulnerability of livingness, that which Giorgio Agamben connects to the stateless refugee, which Mendieta once was. Amidst the Cuban Revolution at age twelve, she was separated from her family and sent to the United States by Operación Pedro Pan. Her body of work feels ecstatically connected and connective: "My art is the way I re-establish the bonds that tie me to the universe."[3]

Mendieta's death occurred during roiling political struggle in the art world. By the 1970s and '80s, conceptualism and semiotic art established itself amidst confrontational, political and performative work. The emerging international market raised all stakes and intensified these differences. A few years earlier, Carolee Schneemann's *Meat Joy* opened new possibilities for the body in art. Its messy, anarchic conglomeration of bodies spoke back to the masculinist culture surrounding abstract expressionism. Conceptual artist and philosopher Adrian

Piper parsed racism by staging social situations that contained real power dynamics. Feminist logic and lexicon cross-pollinated with film theory. Mendieta wrote,

> The US, the greatest imperialist power, rich in material as well as technological resources, maintains some of the most shameful, hurting and inhuman forms of racial, economic and social discriminations amongst its own people. The over-flowing of its frontiers, aggressions and military occupations and colonial and neo-colonial politics of the United States imperialism have denaturalized and violated cultural and artistic tradition of other peoples as well as within the US itself.[4]

Her art challenged hegemonic power; it contested beauty, value and eventually Western spirituality. By the time of her death, Mendieta was deep in an articulated decolonial praxis. Mendieta's murder was imbued with an uncanny feeling. The fight in the 34th floor New York apartment was reportedly about the minimalist, conceptual Andre getting (in his words) "more exposure to the public" than Mendieta.[5]

As a graduate student in 1973 in the Intermedia program at the University of Iowa, Mendieta invited fellow students to her home where they discovered her bent forward over a table with her clothing around her ankles, a messy map of blood drying on her ass and legs. The performance and subsequent photographs of *Untitled (Rape Scene)* were based on the real assault and suffocation of Sarah Ann Ottens, a

20 year old University of Iowa student, in her dorm room the same year.[6] "In the rape pieces," writes Julia Bryan-Wilson, "Mendieta seems to be rehearsing various postures of female subjugation of submission almost as if to exorcise them."[7] Still, this work need not declare, signify, correct, or clean up culture; a space must be cleared for its indeterminacy, its non-productivity. Mendieta played with images of bondage, subjugation, injury, ugliness and a punk sort of communication jamming. In one film she writes, *she got love*, with her bare hands in blood on the side of a white barn, then walks imperviously out of the camera frame.

When Mendieta arrived in Iowa with her older sister in 1961 she got sent to a reform school by dint of a random administrative decision. In the U.S. she experienced racialization for the very first time. Without parents or home, Mendieta eventually reconnected to Cuba through Santería. She had been raised Catholic but absorbed Santerían rituals through the cooks and cleaners who worked in her wealthy family home. At his trial, Andre's lawyer tried to smear Mendieta as a "voodoo practitioner."[8]

At that time, Andre was held aloft by a powerful, influential, and wealthy network of mostly male conceptual artists. Declared Richard Prince, "Lawrence Weiner says Carl didn't have anything to do with her death, and that's enough for me."[9] Andre's clean, formal, gallery-ready work gestures meanings which are inextricable from preexisting international art markets. His linear, architectural pieces get easily coded as value. *Carl Andre: Sculpture as Place* exhibited in 2014 and 2015 at Dia: Beacon. It got disrupted by performances of crying and blood. The Museum of Contemporary Art in Los Angeles exhibited the same show in 2017. A former curator at the museum itself participated in an action against the exhibition. The San Francisco Museum of Modern Art currently displays a room of Andre's sculpture on their fifth floor. Ten of Andre's works are owned in their collections. The Berkeley Art Museum's permanent collection includes six of Andre's artworks. The Tate holds eleven, the Museum of Modern Art, twenty-seven.

Signification in art accrues, accretes, and sediments with time. Andre's geometric materials-focused sculptures have progressed through the art market untouched by the history of his wife's death. However, the trial and the artworld rift infuses their museum presence. Imagining Andre's art otherwise is a fantasy of structural misogyny. When protesters insist, "Dónde Está Ana Mendieta?" or "Where is Ana Mendieta?" they are also asking: where is the work the artist had yet to make? Where is Mendieta's enlivened politics, her social courage? She died at the midpoint of a public art project, *La Jungla*, which was going to be installed in Los Angeles' MacArthur Park. The question for institutions is not just, "Where is Ana Mendieta?" but "How could no new meanings have tethered to Andre's work?"

Dia Art Foundation let several decades pass between Andre's trial and his retrospective; despite this passing of time, the trauma has not passed. The organic language of *healing* is incorrect for social violence, as if one could or would want to return to ignorance of violent social domination. To announce that an Andre exhibit triggers trauma for some (but not for others) is only to announce the most obvious cultural information.

Her Super-8 films depict Mendieta's naked body in a stream, emerging slowly from under a pile of rocks, or as a silhouette of fireworks alight and flickering. Moving at the metabolic pace of prayer or growth, the "earth-body" work such as *Creek* or *Untitled (Burial Pyramid)* manifest the *bare life* of Agamben's writing. At the age of 34 Mendieta described her work this way:

> My art is grounded in the belief of one universal energy which runs through everything: from insect to man, from man to spectre, from spectre to plant from plant to galaxy. My works are the irrigation veins of this universal fluid. Through them ascend the ancestral sap, the original beliefs, the primordial accumulations, the unconscious thought that animates the world. There is no original past to redeem: there is the void, the orphanhood, the unbaptized earth of the beginning, the time that from within the earth looks upon us. There is above all the search for origin.[10]

The work is transformative. Evoking reverent time, the rituals activate the raw materials that form form. Grass, mud, fire, and blood reenchant a cosmological ecology. She explains in an undated artist statement,

"The turning point in my art was in 1972, when I realized that my paintings were not real enough for what I wanted the image to convey, and by real I mean I wanted my images to have power, to be magic." Younger work plays with drag, such as the 1972 *Untitled (Facial Hair Transplants)*, or distorts her face by pressing it against glass, as in *Untitled (Glass on Body Imprints).* Many performances and films use blood. It seeps under the crack in a door in *Moffitt Building Piece*, suggests tragedy in the *Untitled (Self-Portrait with Blood)* which "documents" an imaginary crime, enacts martyrdom as in *Untitled (Sweating Blood)* or religious ritual as in *Untitled (Death of a Chicken)*. These images are at once profane, sacred and traumatic. They connect her to artists who strike a challenge at the point of the social encounter—Vito Acconci, Hans Bellmer, the Viennese Actionists. All of Mendieta's work involves her body. The body reemerges in contemporary art as geopolitical forces exert increasing biopolitical domination over most people.

Mendieta's work is misused in all kind of ways. Mendieta's *Silueta Series* is not "goddess art," but representation of specific Santerían deities. Santería arose amid the situation of surviving enslavement and colonialism.[11] Mendieta's work enacts, in Bryan-Wilson's words, "The borderline nature of the constitutive practice." She says, "One could say that in such work Mendieta moved *contra el cuerpo* (against the body)—in the sense that a counter-attack is a redoubling of effort, and a counter-proposition does not negate the original but seeks to answer it. Just as there is no such thing as 'the earth' or 'the goddess,' there is no such thing as 'the body' in Mendieta's work; she goes against 'the body' to reassert the existence of, and interdependency between, many bodies."[12] The art's traumatic mood includes the trauma of nation and race. Coco Fusco writes, "At the time it seemed that the only way a Latina could gain attention was to die dramatically."[13]

Mendieta's death gets moored to the registers and resonances of the work in ways that sometimes eclipse it. The protective humanist, feminist feelings evoked by the tragedy does not retrospectively make her a Western, first world feminist. The purpose of this transformative work is not to heal, balm, or counter the trauma felt about her death. The collective feminist A.I.R. Gallery exhibited Mendieta's first solo show in 1979. As a member of its Task Force on Discrimination against Women and Minority Artists, she organized an exhibition there of artists from the developing world. Her curatorial statement read, "American feminism as it stands is basically a white middle class movement." Ultimately, Mendieta left A.I.R. stating, "its white, middle-class members were unable or unwilling to address issues of power and diversity in their community."[14] Here is the actual link to feminism: Mendieta's death was a femicide, distinguished from homicide by its inextricability with the victim being gendered female, cis or trans. Reconfigured as such, Mendieta's art or life is not made to stand in for anything beyond itself, and the tragedy of her death is connected across nation and race to a pattern of patriarchal and misogynistic violence.

This situation strains at the Kantian *sensus communis*, or shared common sense. It is useful here to dispense of the imagined totality of an "art world." Just like "patriarchy" is a word, yet also an intricate and interlocking personal and legalistic set of power relations, the "art world" is an imaginary summation. When I visited the San Francisco Museum of Modern Art room full of Andre's work, an older women stood next to me. Together, we silently read the accompanying text on the wall. As if murmuring about the price of produce, I asked her if she knew Andre had killed his wife. She became excited, I was not sure at all what to expect. She told me she was an architect, and that Andre's *Copper-Zinc Plain* was her favorite artwork in the museum. She said she had just been listening to a classical composition and discovered the composer had *also* killed his wife! Is it possible that the narrative of man killing his wife is simply acceptable in the "realm of the sensible" in Western culture? Is the idea that it would *not* belong in the museum the anomaly? Do we fault an institution for upholding a pattern the institution cannot function outside of, a pattern the institution cannot function *without*? The material history of Kant's "disinterested delight" might also reveal the adjacent history of disinterested violence.

This is why the fight must be had and had again. It is not only unsettling gender, or Western, white domination, it is unsettling the authority of the museum, which here enacts all these things. When speaking on the work of artist David Hammons, poet Fred Moten said, "what if whiteness was inside blackness?"[15] I ask, what if the museum was inside art rather than the other way round? What if what counts as spiritual was not inside the museum but the museum was inside the spiritual? This refiguring may lead to a different equation of Andre/Mendieta, which one can easily see was never quite an equation in the first place, but only seemed to act as one by sanding off the most awkwardly obvious immutable difference. But what if we took out the word difference there? What would be inside of what, what imaginary in what reality? I am not a great believer in justice. This is different than saying I do not long for it, or against all evidence to the contrary, like most people, naturally expect it. I prefer the concept of vitality. Through the word vitality, one can think about how things grow, or just continue to live, and how and why in contrast, others do not. Every creative person understands what is necessary to tend to life, to sustain it, to make it grow. What is art's responsibility to vitality? What life, what life's work are these curators (see *curare*, or *cura*, meaning care) fostering? And mimetically, resonantly, or symbolically at the cost of what vitality?

NOTES

The epigraph is from *The Coming Community* by Giorgio Agamben. The book is translated by Michael Hardt and published by the University of Minnesota, 1993.

Time Flows Onto the Highways, Escapes up the Interstate

1. Frank Wilderson, "Untitled Lecture." Lecture, Qilombo Community Center, Oakland, California, February 22, 2015.

2. Elaine Scarry, "Beauty and Social Justice." Lecture, Cambridge University, Cambridge, England, May 21, 2010.

3. Hito Steyerl, *The Wretched of the Screen* (Berlin: Sternberg Press, 2012).

Day and Night

1. Henri Lefebvre, *Rhythmanalysis: Space, Time and Everyday Life* (New York: Continuum, 2004).

2. The "Ellis Act" is a California state law which establishes that landlords have the unconditional right to evict tenants to "go out of business." Most Ellis evictions are used to convert rental units to condominiums, using loopholes in the condo law. https://www.sftu.org/ellis/

3. Christopher D. Cook, "Elderly Family's Eviction Fuels Housing Rights Movement," 10/15/2013, https://www.peoplepowermedia.org/housing/elderly-family%E2%80%99s-eviction-fuels-growing-san-francisco-housing-rights-movement

4. Murray Bush, "Developers' Vision Decision Shoves out Seniors, Artists," December 7, 2013, http://vancouver.mediacoop.ca/photo/developers-vision-decision-shoves-out-seniors-arti/20324

The Plaza

1. Niklas Damiris and Helga Wild, "The Internet: A New Agora?" http://topologicalmedialab.net/xinwei/pub/img/sources/Damiris/Internet-A_New_Agora.pdf

2. Bonney, Sean, "Further Notes on Militant Poetics," September 27, 2013, http://abandonedbuildings.blogspot.com/2013/09/further-notes-on-militant-poetics.html

We cover our girlish faces. We are the war.

1. See the Guatemala Human Rights Commission / USA factsheet, "Femicide and Feminicide," http://www.ghrc-usa.org/wp-content/uploads/2011/12/Femicide-FACTsheet-2013.pdf

2. Saidiya Hartman, *Scenes of Subjection* (Oxford: Oxford University Press, 1997), 92.

3. Rosa-Linda Fregoso and Cynthia Bejarano, eds., *Terrorizing Women: Feminicide in the Americas*,

(Durham, NC: Duke University Press, 2009).

4. Cassandra Troyan, *Post-Sovereign Poetics: Resistance in Traumatic Violence*, "Biopolitical, Post-Sovereignty, Post-Recognition Poetics," Poetics: (The Next) 25 Years Conference, SUNY-University at Buffalo, April 9, 2016

NOTE: *Style* was originally published in Spanish as *Estilo* in 2011, then translated by Jen Hofer for a 2016 bilingual edition.

Reading

1. *I See Infinite Distance Between Any Point and Another* debuted at "dOCUMENTA 13" in 2012 and also exhibited at "Words and Places: Etel Adnan," 2013, Wattis Institute for Contemporary Arts.

2. Kaja Silverman, *The Acoustic Mirror: The Female Voice in Psychoanalysis and Cinema* (Bloomington, IN: Indiana University Press, 1988).

3. Giorgio Agamben, *The Coming Community*, trans. Michael Hardt (Minneapolis, MN: University of Minnesota, 1993).

Being Desire

1. Micha Cárdenas, "Dark Shimmers: The Rhythm of Necropolitical Affect in Digital Media," in *Trap Door: Trans Cultural Production and the Politics of Visibility*, eds. Reina Gossett, Eric A. Stanley, and Johanna Burton (Cambridge, MA: The MIT Press,

2017), 161-3.

2. "gesture is a gender / a shining bracelet which amplifies a slim wrist." *The Capilano Review* 3, no. 9 (Summer 2017): 12-13.

3. Hito Steyerl, *The Wretched of the Screen* (Berlin: Sternberg Press, 2012).

4. Gilles Deleuze and Felix Guattari, *Kafka: Toward a Minor Literature* (Minneapolis, MN: University of Minnesota Press, 1986).

5. Andria Nyberg, "On Sublimity and the Excessive Object in Trans Women's Contemporary Writing," Södertörns University Master's Thesis, 2015. Here, Nyberg is quoting Barbara Claire Freeman from *The Feminine Sublime: Gender and Excess in Women's Fiction* (UC Press, 1997).

6. Hélène Cixous, "The Laugh of the Medusa," *Signs: Journal of Women in Culture and Society*, Vol. 1, No. 4 (Summer 1975): 873-93.

The Communicative Community

Alphonzo Lingis, *The Community of Those Who Have Nothing in Common*, (Bloomington, IN: Indiana University Press, 1994).

Jodi Dean, "Communicative Capitalism: Circulation and the Foreclosure of Politics," in *Cultural Politics: An International Journal*, 2005.

Lisa Robertson, *Nilling* (Toronto: Bookthug, 2012).

Round

1. Giorgio Agamben, *The Coming Community*, trans. Michael Hardt (Minneapolis, MN: University of Minnesota, 1993).

2. Jacques Rancière, "Shifting Borders: Art, Politics and Ethics Today," Lecture, Rhetoric Spring Colloquium at University of California, Berkeley, Berkeley, California, February 20, 2018.

3. Kaja Silverman, *The Acoustic Mirror: The Female Voice in Psychoanalysis and Cinema* (Bloomington, IN: Indiana University Press, 1988).

4. "The technology works by analyzing the physical and behavioral features that make each person's voice distinctive, such as the pitch, shape of the mouth, and length of the larynx. An algorithm then creates a dynamic computer model of the individual's vocal characteristics. This is what's popularly referred to as a 'voiceprint'…Although the NSA is known to rely on finger and face prints to identify targets, voiceprints, according to a 2008 agency document, are 'where NSA reigns supreme.'" Ava Kofman, "Finding Your Voice," *The Intercept*, January 19, 2018, https://theintercept.com/2018/01/19/voice-recognition-technology-nsa/

What Imaginary Thing is a Museum?

1. Filippo Tomasi Marinetti, “The Futurist Manifesto” (Paris: Figaro, 1909) accessed at https://www.societyforasianart.org/sites/default/files/manifesto_futurista.pdf

2. Howard Oransky, ed., *Covered in Time and History: The Films of Ana Mendieta* (Berkeley: University of California Press, 2015).

3. Ana Mendieta, unpublished artist statement, 1981.

4. Ana Mendieta, “The Struggle for Culture Today Is the Struggle for Life,” in *Ana Mendieta*, ed. Gloria Moure (Barcelona: Ediciones Poligrafa, 1996), 175.

5. Ronald Sullivan, “Greenwich Village Sculptor Acquitted of Pushing Wife to Her Death,” *New York Times*, February 12, 1988, http://www.nytimes.com/1988/02/12/nyregion/greenwich-village-sculptor-acquitted-of-pushing-wife-to-her-death.html

6. http://www.iowaunsolvedmurders.com/beyond-1965-selected-unsolved-iowa-murders/spring-break-killer-murder-of-sarah-ann-ottens-1973/

7. Julia Bryan-Wilson, “Against the Body,” *Ana Mendieta: Traces* (London: Hayward Publishing, 2014).

8. B. Ruby Rich, “The Films of Ana Mendieta: Panel Discussion,” BAMPFA, January 28, 2017.

9. Richard Prince, “Birdtalk,” http://www.richardprince.com/birdtalk/

10. Ana Mendieta, “A Selection of Statements and Notes,” *Sulfur*, vol. 22, 1988, 70.

11. The references might also be considered research-based, playful, meaningful, masterful, like Robert Smithson's geography in Monuments of Passaic (1967). "Strictly speaking," says critic Abigail Solomon-Godeau, "ritual requires communal participation, temporal repetition, and (not least) religious belief...whatever her affinities to or appropriations of particular traditions, Mendieta's actions and performances are...functioning therefore, not 'authentically' but mimetically, indeed, performatively." Abigail Solomon-Godeau, ed., "Ana Mendieta without Atavism," *Ana Mendieta: Blood & Fire* (Paris: Galerie Lelong, 2011).

12. Julia Bryan-Wilson, "Against the Body," *Ana Mendieta: Traces* (London: Hayward Publishing, 2014).

13. Jared Quinton, "Coco Fusco on the Enduring Legacy of Groundbreaking Cuban Artist Ana Mendieta," *Artsy*, Feburary 3, 2016. https://www.artsy.net/article/artsy-editorial-ana-mendieta-s-enduring-legacy-in-the-words-of-coco-fusco

14. Karen Fiss, "Karen Fiss on Ana Mendieta," *Open Space*, February 6, 2012. https://openspace.sfmoma.org/2012/02/fiss-on-mendieta/

15. Fred Moten, Untitled Lecture, The Wattis Institute for Contemporary Arts, March 10, 2017.

IMAGE CREDITS

Stephanie Syjuco, *The Precariat (Material Witnesses)*, 2013, Installation View. Courtesy of the artist and Catherine Clark Gallery, San Francisco.

Noah Berger, Untitled photograph of a Berkeley, California, highway shutdown, 2015.

Lynne Sachs, *Your Day is My Night*, film still, 2012.

Stephanie Syjuco, *The Precariat (Material Witnesses)*, 2013, installation view.

Geoffrey Farmer, *SFAI Fountain*, 2017; Installation view, *A way out of the mirror*, Canada Pavilion, 57th Venice Biennale, Venice, Italy. Photo: Francesco Barasciutti. Courtesy of Catriona Jeffries, Vancouver.

"8.—We came to visit your bed. A cluster of girls. Everything was very ambiguous. Everything was bloodless. We came. To approach you. To find your hands ready for torture. To stain you for when you wake. We are a cluster of girls playing at kissing each other. Taking you by the hands. Dazzle. We aren't doing anything bad. We are not pain not exhaustion not death."

Dolores Dorantes, *Style* trans. Jen Hofer (Chicago: Kenning Editions, 2016), photographs by author.

Anaïs Nin, *The Diary of Anaïs Nin Volume One: 1931-1934* (New York: Harcourt Brace Jovanovich, 1931-1974).

BREAST BUTTER SOFT,
GLOSSY GLASSY

BUT I SPEAK WELL,
THEY CALL ME ASHLEY

THEN I CALLED ON GOD,
HE CALLED ME ASHY

Juliana Huxtable, *Mucus in My Pineal Gland* (New York: Wonder, 2017), photographs by author (with Jess Horn).

The Otolith Group, *I See Infinite Distance Between Any Point and Another*, 2012; installation shot from Words and Places: Etel Adnan, 2013, at CCA Wattis Institute for Contemporary Arts. Photo by the author.

Janet Cardiff, *The Forty Part Motet*, 2001, Installation View (detail), Gallery 308, Fort Mason Center for Arts & Culture, 2015. Courtesy of Fort Mason Center for Arts & Culture, San Francisco, and San Francisco Museum of Modern Art. Photo: JKA Photography.

Photograph by the author, 2018.

PUBLICATION CREDITS

"Time Flows Onto the Highways, Escapes up the Interstate," *New Media Art 2017: Back to Nature*, Cica Museum, Gimpo, Korea, 2017.

"What Imaginary Thing is a Museum?" *Art Practical*, May 4, 2017.

"Day and Night," originally published as, "Your Day is My Night," *Open Space,* the San Francisco Museum of Modern Art's interdisciplinary arts and culture platform, 2014.

"The Plaza," originally published as, "SECA 2012: Anne Lesley Selcer on Frank Ogawa Plaza," *Open Space*, 2013.

"We cover our girlish faces. We are the war." *Jacket2*, 2018.

"Trauma is a Memory with the Roof Blown Off," *Open Space*, 2017.

"Reading," *Open Space*, 2013.

"Love," *Doppelganger Magazine*, 2006.

"Being Desire," *Jacket2*, 2018.

"The Communicative Community," *The Chicago Review* Issue 59:01/02, "Gender Forum," 2015.

"Round," *Art Practical*, March 13, 2018.

Thank you Jacob Kahn, Justin Carder, Valerie Imus, Patricia Maloney, Genevieve Quick, Southern Exposure and Wolfman Books. Thanks to the curatorial committee that created the Art Writing Fellowship which enabled this book. Thank you to every editor of each publication in which these essays were formerly published. Thanks to Sitka and Yvan. Thank you to every artist in this book <3